THE SEVEN DEADLY SINNES
OF LONDON
BY THOMAS DEKKER

THE

Seuen Deadly Sinnes

of London :

Drawne in seuen seuerall Coaches,
Through the seuen seuerall Gates of the
Citie

Bringing the Plague with them.

Opus septem Dierum.

Tho: Dekker.

At London
Printed by *E. A.* for *Nathaniel Butter,* and are to bee sold
at his shop neere Saint Austens gate.
1606.

CAMBRIDGE UNIVERSITY PRESS
Cambridge, New York, Melbourne, Madrid, Cape Town,
Singapore, São Paulo, Delhi, Mexico City

Cambridge University Press
The Edinburgh Building, Cambridge CB2 8RU, UK

Published in the United States of America by Cambridge University Press, New York

www.cambridge.org
Information on this title: www.cambridge.org/9781107634404

First published 1905
First paperback edition 2013

A catalogue record for this publication is available from the British Library

ISBN 978-1-107-63440-4 Paperback

The 1905 edition of this publication was printed on hand-made paper
using the Cambridge type. 225 copies were made available for sale.

Reader,

IT is as ordinarie a custome (for vs that are Bookish) to haue a bout with thee, after wee haue done with a Patron, as for Schollers (in the noble Science) to play at the woodden Rapier and Dagger at the ende of a Maisters prize. In doing which we know not vpon what Speeding points wee runne, for you (that are Readers) are the most desperate and fowlest players in the world, you will strike when a mans backe is toward you, and kill him (if you could for shame) when he lies vnder your feete. You are able (if you haue the tokens of deadly Ignorance, and Boldnes at one time vpon you) to breede more infection on in Pauls Church-yard, then all the bodies that were buried there in the Plague-time, if they had beene left still aboue ground. You stand somtimes at a Stationers stal, looking scuruily (like Mules champing vpon Thistles) on the face of a new Booke

3 a 2

bee it neuer so worthy: and goe (as il
fauouredly) mewing away: But what get
you by it? The Booke-seller euer after
when you passe by, pinnes on your backes
the badge of fooles to make you be laught
to scorne, or of sillie Carpers to make you
be pittied: Conradus Gesner neuer writ of
the nature of such strange beasts as you
are: for where as we call you Lectores,
Readers, you turne your selues into Lictores,
Executioners, and tormenters. I wold not
haue him that writes better than I, to Reade
this, nor him that cannot doe so well, to
Raile, or if hee cannot chuse but Raile, let
him doe it to my face: otherwise (to me
being absent) it is done cowardly: for
Leonem mortuum mordent etiam Catuli:
Cats dare scratch Lions by the face when
they lie dead, and none but Colliers will
threaten a Lord Maior when they are
farre enough from the Cittie. I haue
laide no blockes in thy way: if
thou findest Strawes,
(Vade, vale,) caue ne titubes.

The names of the Actors in this
old Enterlude of Iniquitie.

1 Politike Banke-
  ruptisme.

2 Lying.

3 Candle-light.

4 Sloth.   Seuen may easily play
                  this, but not without
5 Apishnesse.   a Diuell.

6 Shauing.

7 Crueltie.

To the Worshipfull and very worthy
Gentleman Henry Fermor Es-
quire, Clarke of the Peace for the
Countie of Middlesex.

I AM sory (deare Sir) that in a time (so
abundant with wit) I shold send vnto you
no better fruit then the sins of a City : but
they are not common, (for they were neuer
gathered till this yeare) and therefore I send
them for the Rarity : Yet now I remember
my selfe, they are not the Sinnes of a Citie,
but onely the picture of them. And a
Drollerie (or Dutch peece of Lantskop) may
sometimes breed in the beholders eye, as
much delectation, as the best and most
curious master-peece excellent in that Art.
Bookes being sent abroad after they are
begotten into the world, as This of mine is,
are in the nature of Orphans ; But being
receiued into a Gardianship (as I make
no doubt but this shall) they come into the

happie state of adopted children. That office must now be yours, and you neede not bee ashamed of it, for Kings haue beene glad to doe them honour, that haue bestowed such a neuer-dying honour vppon them. The benefite you shall receiue, is this, that you see the building vp of a tombe (in your life time) wherein you are sure so to lie, as that you cannot bee forgotten; and you read that very Epitaph that shal stand ouer you, which by no Enuie can bee defaced, nor by any time worne out. I haue made choise of you alone, to bee the onely Patron to these my labours: by which word (onely) I chalenge to my selfe a kinde of Dignitie: for there hath beene a Generation of a sort of strange fellowes (and I thinke the race is not yet eaten out) who when a Booke (of theire owne) hath bin borne in the lawfull Matrimonie of Learning, and Industrie, haue basely compeld it either like a bastard, to call a great many father (and to goe vnder all their names) or else (like a common fellow at a Sessions) to put himselfe (as the tearme is) vpon twelue godfathers. In which case (contrarie to all law) the Foreman is most dishonoured. That art of Skeldring I studie not, I stand vpon stronger Bases.

7

The current of a mans Reputation, being diuided into so manie Riuolets must needes grow weake. If you giue intertainment to this in your best affection, you will binde me (one day) to heighten your name, when by some more worthy Columne (by me to be erected) I shall consecrate that and your selfe to an euerlasting and sacred Memorie.

Most affectionately desirous
to be yours:

Tho. Dekker.

The Induction to the Booke.

I FINDE it written in that Booke where no vntruthes can be read : in that Booke whose leaues shall out-last sheetes of brasse, and whose lynes leade to eternity: yea euen in that Booke that was pend by the best Author of the best wisedome, allowed by a Deity, licensed by the Omnipotent, and published (in all Languages to all Nations) by the greatest, truest, and onely Diuine, thus I find it written, that for Sinne, Angels were throwne out of heauen; for Sinne, the first man that euer was made, was made an outcast: he was driuen out of his liuing that was left vnto him by his Creator: It was a goodlier liuing, than the Inheritance of Princes: he lost Paradice by it (he lost his house of pleasure:) hee lost Eden by it, a Garden, where Winter could neuer haue nipt him with cold, nor Summer haue scorcht him with heate. He had there all fruits growing to delight his taste, all flowers flourishing to allure his eye, all Birds singing to content his eare; he had more than he could desire: yet because he desired more than was fit for him, he lost all. For Sinne, all those buildings which that greate Worke-master of the world had in sixe dayes raysed, were swallowed at the first by waters, and shall at last be consumed in fire. How many families hath this Leuiathan deuoured? how many Cities? how many Kingdoms? Let vs awhile leaue Kingdomes, and enter into Cities. Sodom and Gomorrah were burnt to the ground with brimstone that dropt in flakes from heauen: a hot and dreadfull vengeance. Ierusalem hath not a stone left vpon another of her first glorious foundation: a heauy and fearefull downefall. Ierusalem, that was Gods owne dwelling house; the Schoole where those Hebrew Lectures, which he himselfe read, were taught; the very Nursery where the Prince of Heauen was brought vp; that Ierusalem, whose Rulers were Princes, and whose Citizens were like the sonnes of Kings: whose Temples were paued with gold, and whose houses stood like rowes of tall Cedars; that Ierusalem is now a dezert; It is vnhallowed, and vntrodden: no Monument is left to shew it was a Citty, but only the memoriall of the Iewes hard-hartednes, in making away their Sauiour: It is now a place for barbarous Turks, and poore despised Grecians; it is rather now (for the abominations committed in it) no place at all.

Let vs hoyst vp more Sayles, and lanch into other Seas, till wee come in ken of our owne Countrey. Antwerp (the eldest daughter of Brabant) hath falne in her pride, the Citties of rich Burgundy in theyr greatnes. Those seuenteene Dutch Virgins of Belgia, (that had Kingdomes to theyr dowries, and were worthy to be courted by Nations) are now no more Virgins: the Souldier hath deflowred them, and robd them of theyr Mayden honor: Warre hath still vse of their noble bodyes, and discouereth theyr nakednes like prostituted Strumpets. Famine hath dryed vp the fresh bloud in theyr cheekes, whilst the Pestilence digd vp theyr Fields, and turned them into Graues. Neither haue these punishments bin layd vpon them onely; for bloud hath bin also drawne of their very next neighbours. France lyes yet panting vnder the blowes which her owne Children haue giuen her. Thirty yeeres together suffred she her bowels to be torne out by those that were bred within them: She was full of Princes, and saw them all lye mangled at her feete: She was full of people, and saw in one night a hundred thousand massacred in her streetes: her Kings were eaten vp by Ciuill warres, and her Subiects by fire and famine. O gallant Monarchy, what hard fate hadst thou, that when none were left to conquer thee, thou shouldst triumph ouer thy selfe! Thou hast Wynes flowing in thy veynes: but thou madest thy selfe druncke with thine owne bloud. The English, the Dutch, and the Spanish, stoode aloofe and gaue ayme, whilst thou shotst arrowes vpright, that fell vpon thine owne head, and wounded thee to death. Wouldst thou (and the rest) know the reason, why your bones haue bin bruzed with rods of Iron? It was, because you haue risen in Arch-rebellion against the Supremest Soueraigne: You haue bin Traytors to your Lord, the King of heauen and earth, and haue armed your selues to fight against the Holy Land. Can the father of the world measure out his loue so vnequally, that one people (like to a mans yongest child) should be more made of than all the rest, being more

12

vnruly than the rest? O London, thou art great in glory, and enuied for thy greatnes: thy Towers, thy Temples, and thy Pinnacles stand vpon thy head like borders of fine gold, thy waters like frindges of siluer hang at the hemmes of thy garments. Thou art the goodliest of thy neighbors, but the prowdest; the welthiest, but the most wanton. Thou hast all things in thee to make thee fairest, and all things in thee to make thee foulest; for thou art attir'de like a Bride, drawing all that looke vpon thee, to be in loue with thee, but there is much harlot in thine eyes. Thou sitst in thy Gates heated with Wines, and in thy Chambers with lust. What miseries haue of late ouertaken thee? yet (like a foole that laughs when hee is putting on fetters) thou hast bin merry in height of thy misfortunes. She (that for almost halfe a hundred of yeeres) of thy Nurse became thy Mother, and layd thee in her bosome, whose head was full of cares for thee, whilst thine slept vpon softer pillowes than downe. She that wore thee alwayes on her brest as the richest Iewell in her kingdome, who had continually her eye vpon thee, and her heart with thee: whose chaste hand clothed thy Rulers in

Qu. Elizabeths death.

13

Scarlet, and thy Inhabitants in roabes of peace: euen she was taken from thee, when thou wert most in feare to lose her: when thou didst tremble (as at an earth-quake) to thinke that bloud should runne in thy Channels, that the Canon should make way through thy Portcullises, and fire rifle thy wealthy houses, then, euen then wert thou left full of teares, and becamst an Orphan. But behold, thou hadst not sat many howres on the banks of King Iames his Coronation. sorrow, but thou hadst a louing Father that adopted thee to be his owne: thy mourning turnd presently to gladnes, thy terrors into triumphs. Yet, lest this fulnesse of ioy should beget in thee a wantonnes, and to try how wisely thou couldst take vp affliction, Sicknes was sent to breathe her vnwholsome ayres into thy nosthrils, so that thou, that wert before the only Gallant and Minion of the world, hadst in a short time more diseases (then a common Harlot hath) hanging vpon thee; thou suddenly becamst the by-talke of neighbors, the scorne and contempt of Nations.

Heere could I make thee weepe thy selfe away into waters, by calling back those sad and dismall houres, wherein

thou consumedst almost to nothing with
shrikes and lamentations, in that
*Wonderfull yeere, when these
miserable calamities entred in
at thy Gates, slaying 30000. and
more as thou heldst them in
thine armes, but they are fresh
in thy memory, and the story of them (but
halfe read ouer) would strike so coldly to
thy heart, and lay such heauy sorrow vpon
mine (Namque animus meminisse horret,
luctuque refugit) that I will not be thine
and my owne tormentor with the memory
of them.   How quickly notwithstanding
didst thou forget that beating? The wrath
of him that smot thee, was no sooner
(in meere pitty of thy stripes) appeased,
but howrely (againe) thou wert in the
company of euill doers, euen before thou
couldst finde leysure to aske him for-
giuenes.

Euer since that time hath hee winckt at
thy errors, and suffred thee (though now
thou art growne old, and lookest very
ancient) to goe on still in the follyes of
thy youth : he hath ten-fold restor'de thy
lost sonnes and daughters, and such sweete,
liuely, fresh colours hath hee put vpon thy
cheekes, that Kings haue come to behold

*A Booke so
called, written
by the Author,
describing the
horror of the
Plague in 1602,
when there
dyed 30578. of
that disease.

thee, and Princes to delight their eyes with thy bewty. None of all these fauours (for all this) can draw thee from thy wickednes:

Graces haue powred downe out of heauen vpon thee, and thou art rich in all things, sauing in goodnes: So that now once againe hath he gone about (and but gone about) to call thee to the dreadfull Barre of his Iudgement. And no maruaile: for whereas other Citties (as glorious as thy selfe,) and other people (as deare vnto him as thine) haue in his indignation bin quite taken from the face of the earth, for some one peculiar Sinne, what hope hast thou to grow vp still in the pride of thy strength, gallantnes and health, hauing seuen deadly and detestable sinnes lying night by night by thy lasciuious sides? O thou beawtifullest daughter of two vnited Monarchies! from thy womb receiued I my being, from thy brests my nourishment; yet giue me leaue to tell thee, that thou hast seuen Diuels within thee, and till they be cleane cast out, the Arrowes of Pestilence will fall vpon thee by day, and the hand of the Inuader strike thee by night. The Sunne will shine, but not be a comfort to thee, and the Moone

16

looke pale with anger, when she giues thee light. Thy Louers will disdayne to court thee: thy Temples will no more send out Diuine oracles: Iustice will take her flight, and dwell else-where; and that Desolation, which now for three yeeres together hath houered round about thee, will at last enter, and turne thy Gardens of pleasure, into Church-yards; thy Fields that seru'd thee for walks, into Golgotha; and thy hye built houses, into heapes of dead mens Sculs. I call him to witnes, who is all Truth, I call the Cittizens of heauen to witnes, who are all spotlesse, that I slander thee not, in saying thou nourishest seuen Serpents at thy brests, that will destroy thee: let all thy Magistrates and thy officers speake for me: let Strangers that haue but seene thy behauiour, be my Iudges: let all that are gathered vnder thy wings, and those that sleepe in thy bosome, giue their verdict vpon me; yea, try me (as thy brabblings are) by all thy Petit and Graund Iurors, and if I belye thee, let my Country (when I expire) deny me her common bless-ing, Buriall. Lift vp therefore thy head (thou Mother of so many people:) awaken out of thy dead and dangerous slumbers, and with a full and fearelesse eye behold those

seuen Monsters, that with extended iawes
gape to swallow vp thy memory : for I will
into so large a field single euery one of
them, that thou and all the world shall see
their vglinesse, for by seeing them, thou
mayst auoyd them, and by auoyding
them, be the happiest and
most renowned
of Citties.

Politick Bankruptisme,

Or,

The first dayes Triumph
of the first Sinne.

IT is a custome in all Countries, when great personages are to be entertained, to haue great preparation made for them : and because London disdaines to come short of any City, either in Magnificence, State, or expences vpon such an occasion, solemne order was set downe, and seuen seuerall solemne dayes were appointed to receiue these seuen Potentates : for they carry the names of Princes on the earth, and wheresoe're they inhabit, in a short time are they Lords of great Dominions.

The first dayes Triumphs were spent in meeting and conducting Politick Bank-ruptisme into the Freedome : to receiue

whom, the Master, the Keepers, and all
the Prisoners of Ludgate in their
The maner
how Bank-
ruptisme is
entertained,
and at what
Gate.
best clothes stood most offi-
ciously readie: for at that Gate,
his Deadlinesse challenges a
kind of prerogatiue by the Custome of the Citie, and there loues he most
to be let in. The thing they stood vpon,
was a Scaffold erected for the purpose,
stuck round about with a few greene
boughes (like an Alehouse booth at a
Fayre) and couered with two or three threed-
bare Carpets (for prisoners haue no better)
to hide the vnhandsomnes of the Car-
penters worke : the boughes with the very
strong breath that was prest out of the
vulgar, withered, and like Autumnian
leaues dropt to the ground, which made
the Broken Gentleman to hasten his pro-
gresse the more, and the rather, because
Lud and his two sonnes stood in a very
cold place, waiting for his comming. Being
vnder the gate, there stood one arm'd with
an extemporall speech, to giue him the
onset of his welcome : It was not (I would
you should well know) the Clarke of a
country parish, or the Schoolemaster of
a corporate towne, that euery yeere has
a saying to Master Maior, but it was a

bird pickt out of purpose (amongst the Ludgathians) that had the basest and lowest voice, and was able in a Terme time, for a throat, to giue any prisoner great ods for the box at the grate: this Organ pipe was funde to rore for the rest, who with a hye sound and glib deliuery, made an Encomiastick Paradoxicall Oration in praise of a prison, prouing, that captiuity was the only blessing that could happen to man, and that a Politick Bankrupt (because he makes himselfe for euer by his owne wit) is able to liue in any common wealth, and deserues to go vp the ladder of promotion, when fiue hundred shallowpated feollowes shall be turnd off. The poore Orator hauing made vp his mouth, Bankruptisme gaue him very good words, and a handful or two of thanks, vowing he would euer liue in his debt. At which, all the prisoners rending the ayre with shouts, the key was turnd, and vp (in state) was he led into king Luds house of Bondage, to suruey the building, and to take possession of the lodgings; where he no sooner entred, but a lusty peale of welcomes was shot out of Kannes in stead of Canons, and though the powder was exceeding wet, yet off they

Solamen miseris socios habuisse doloris.

went thick and threefold. The day was proclaymed Holiday in all the wardes; euery prisoner swore if he would stay amongst them, they would take no order about their debts, because they would lye by it too; and for that purpose swarmd about him like Bees about Comfit-makers, and were drunke, according to all the learned rules of Drunkennes, as Vpsy-Freeze, Crambo, Parmizant, &c. the pimples of this ranck and full-humord ioy rising thus in their faces, because they all knew, that though he himselfe was broken, the linings of his bags were whole; and though he had no conscience (but a crackt one) yet he had crownes that were sound. None of all these hookes could fasten him to them: he was (like their clocks) to strike in more places than one, and though he knew many Citizens hated him, and that if he were encountred by some of them, it might cost him deere, yet vnder so good a protection did he go (as he said) because he owed no ill will euen to those that most sought his vndoing; and therefore tooke his leaue of the house, with promise, to be with them, or send to them once euery quarter at the
least. So that now, by his wise instructions, if a Puny were

Misery makes men cunning.

22

there amongst them, he might learne more cases, and more quiddits in law within seuen dayes, than he does at his Inne in fourteene moneths.

The Politician beeing thus got into the City, caries himself so discreetly, that he steales into the hearts of many: In words, is he circumspect: in lookes, graue: in attire, ciuill: in diet, temperate: in company affable; in his affaires His qualities. serious: and so cunningly dooes he lay on these colours, that in the end he is welcome to, and familiar with the best. So that now, there is not any one of all the twelue Companies, in which (at one time or other) there are not those that haue forsaken their owne Hall, · to be free of his: yea some of your best Shop-keepers hath he enticed to shut themselues vp from the cares and busines of the world, to liue a priuate life; nay, there is not any great and famous Streete in the City, wherein there hath not (or now doth not) dwell, some one, or other, that hold the points of his Religion. For you must vnderstand, that the Politick Bankrupt is a His disguises. Harpy that lookes smoothly, a Hyena that enchants subtilly, a Mermaid that sings sweetly, and a Cameleon, that

can put himselfe into all colours. Sometimes hee's a Puritane, he sweares by
nothing but Indeede, or rather does not
sweare at all, and wrapping his crafty
Serpents body in the cloake of Religion,
he does those acts that would become none
but a Diuell. Sometimes hee's a Protestant,
and deales iustly with all men, till he see
his time, but in the end he turnes Turke.
Because you shall beleeue me, I will giue
you his length by the Scale, and Anatomize
his body from head to foote.   Heere it is.
Whether he be a Tradesman, or a Mar-
His policy.   chant, when he first sets himselfe vp, and seekes to get the
world into his hands, (yet not to go out of the
City) or first talks of Countries he neuer saw
(vpon the Change) he will be sure to keepe his
dayes of payments more truly, then Lawyers
keepe their Termes, or than Executors
keepe the last lawes that the dead inioyned
them to, which euen Infidels themselues
will not violate : his hand goes to his head,
to his meanest customer, (to expresse his
humilitie ;) he is vp earlier then a Sarieant,
and downe later then a Constable, to proclaime his thrift. By such artificiall
wheeles as these, he winds himselfe vp
into the height of rich mens fauors, till he

grow rich himselfe, and when he sees that they dare build upon his credit, knowing the ground to be good, he takes vpon him the condition of an Asse, to any man that will loade him with gold; and vseth his credit like a Ship freighted with all sorts of Merchandise by ventrous Pilots: for after he hath gotten into his hands so much of other mens goods or money, as will fill him to the vpper deck, away he sayles with it, and politickly runnes him-selfe on ground, to make the world beleeue he had sufferd shipwrack. Then flyes he out like an Irish rebell, and keepes aloofe, hiding his head, when he cannot hide his shame: and though he haue fethers on his back puld from sundry birds, yet to him-selfe is he more wretched, then the Cuckoo in winter, that dares not be seene. The troupes of honest Citizens (his creditors) with whom he hath broken league and hath thus defyed, muster themselues to-gether, and proclaime open warre: their bands consist of tall Yeomen, that serue on foot, commanded by certaine Serieants of their bands, who for leading of men, are knowne to be of more experience then the best Low-country Captaines. In Am-buscado do these lye day and night, to cut off this enemy to the City, if he dare but come downe. But the politick Bankrupt barricadoing his Sconce with double locks, treble dores, inuincible bolts, and pieces of timber 4. or 5. storyes hye, victuals him-selfe for a moneth or so; and then in the dead of night, marches vp higher into the country with bag and baggage: parlies then are summond; compositions offred; a truce is sometimes taken for 3. or 4. yeeres; or (which is more common) a dishonorable peace (seeing no other remedy) is on both sides concluded, he (like the States) being the only gayner by such ciuill warres, whilst the Citizen that is the lender, is the loser: Nam crimine ab vno disce omnes, looke how much he snatches from one mans sheafe, hee gleanes from euery one, if they bee a hundred.

The victory being thus gotton by basenes and trechery, back comes he marching with spred colours againe to the City; aduances in the open streete as he did before; sels the goods of his neighbor before his face without blushing: he iets vp and downe in silks wouen out of other mens stocks, feeds deliciously vpon other mens purses, rides on his ten pound Geldings, in other mens saddles, and is now a new man made out of wax, thats to say, out of those bonds, whose seales he most dishonestly hath canceld. O veluet-garded Theeues! O yea-and-by-nay Cheaters! O ciuill, ô Graue and Right Worshipfull Couzeners!

What a wretchednes is it, by such steps to clime to a counterfetted happines? So to be made for euer, is to be vtterly vndone for euer: So for a man to saue himselfe, is to venture his own damnation; like those that laboring by all meanes to escape ship-wrack, do afterwards desperatly drown themselues. But alas! how rotten at the bottom are buildings thus raised! How soone do such leases grow out of date! The Third House to them is neuer heard of. What slaues then doth mony (so purchast) make of those, who by such wayes thinke to find out perfect freedome? But they are most truly miserable in midst of their ioyes: for their neighbors scorne them, Strangers poynt at them, good men neglect them, the rich man will no more trust them, the begger in his rage vp-braydes them. Yet if this were all, this all were nothing. O thou that on thy pillow (lyke a Spider in his loome) weauest mis-cheuous nets, beating thy braynes, how by casting downe others, to rayse vp thy selfe!

Thou Politick Bankrupt, poore rich man, thou ill-painted foole, when thou art to lye in thy last Inne (thy loathsome graue) how heauy a loade will thy wealth bee to thy weake corrupted Conscience! those heapes of Siluer, in telling of which thou hast worne out thy fingers ends, will be a passing bell, tolling in thine eare, and calling thee to a fearefull Audit. Thou canst not dispose of thy riches, but the naming of euery parcell will strike to thy heart, worse then the pangs of thy departure: thy last will, at the last day, will be an Inditement to cast thee; for thou art guilty of offending those two lawes (enacted in the vpper House of heauen) which directly forbid thee to steale, or to couet thy neighbors goods.

But this is not all neither; for thou lyest on thy bed of death, and art not carde for: thou goest out of the world, and art not lamented: thou art put into the last linnen that euer thou shalt weare, (thy winding-sheete) with reproch, and art sent into thy Graue with curses: he that makes thy Funerall Sermon, dares not speake well of thee, because he is asham'd to belye the dead: and vpon so hatefull a fyle doest thou hang the records of thy life, that euen when the wormes haue pickt thee to the bare bones, those that goe ouer thee, will set vpon thee no Epitaph but this, Here lyes a knaue.

Alack! this is not the worst neither: thy Wife being in the heate of her youth, in the pride of her beawty, and in all the brauery of a rich London Widow, flyes from her nest (where she was thus fledg'd before her time) the City, to shake off the imputation of a Bankrupts Wife, and perhaps marries with some Gallant: thy bags then are emptied, to hold him vp in riots: those hundreds, which thou subtilly tookst vp vpon thy bonds, do sinfully serue him to pay Tauerne bills, and what by knauery thou gotst from honest men, is as villanously spent vpon Pandars and Whores: thy Widow being thus brought to a low ebbe, grows desperat: curses her birth, her life, her fortunes, yea perhaps curses thee, when thou art in thy euerlasting sleepe, her conscience perswading strongly, that she is punished from aboue, for thy faults: and being poore, friendlesse, comfortlesse, she findes no meanes to raise her selfe, but by Falling, and therfore growes to be a common woman. Doth not the thought of this torment thee?

She liues basely by the abuse of that body, to maintaine which in costly garments, thou didst wrong to thine owne soule: nay more to afflict thee, thy children are ready to beg their bread in that very place, where the father hath sat at his dore in purple, and at his boord like Diues, surfeting on those dishes which were earnd by the sweat of other mens browes. The infortunate Marchant, whose estate is swallowed vp by the mercilesse Seas, and the prouident Trades-man, whom riotous Seruants at home, or hard-hearted debters abroad vndermine and ouerthrow, blotting them with the name of Bankrupts, deserue to be pitied and relieued, when thou that hast cozend euen thine owne Brother of his Birth-right, art laught at, and not remembred, but in scorne, when thou art plagued in thy Generation.

Be wise therefore, you Graue, and wealthy Cittizens; play with these Whales of the Sea, till you escape them that are deuourers of your Merchants; hunt these English Wolues to death, and rid the land of them: for these are the Rats that eate vp the prouision of the people: these are the Grashoppers of Egypt, that spoyle the Corne-fields of the Husbandman and the

rich mans Vineyards : they will haue poore
Naboths piece of ground from him, though
they eate a piece of his heart for it. These
are indeede (and none but these) the For-
reners that liue without the freedome of
your City, better than you within it; they
liue without the freedome of honesty, of conscience, and of christianitie. Ten dicing-
houses cheate not yong Gentlemen of so
much mony in a yeare, as these do you in
a moneth. The theefe that dyes at Tyburne
for a robbery, is not halfe so dangerous
a weede in a Common-wealth, as the Politick
Bankrupt. I would there were a Derick to
hang vp him too.

The Russians haue an excellent custome :
they beate them on the shinnes, that haue
mony, and will not pay their debts; if that
law were well cudgeld from thence into
England, Barbar-Surgeons might in a few
yeeres build vp a Hall for their Company,
larger then Powles, only with the cure of
Bankrupt broken-shinnes.

I would faine see a prize set vp, that the
welfed Vsurer, and the politick Bankrupt
might rayle one against another for it :
ô, it would beget a riming Comedy. The
Challenge of the Germayne against all the
Masters of the Noble Science, would not

bring in a quarter of the money: for there is not halfe so much loue betweene the Iron and the Loadestone, as there is mortall hate betweene those two Furies. The Vsurer liues by the lechery of mony, and is Bawd to his owne bags, taking a fee, that they may ingender. The Politick Bankrupt liues by the gelding of bags of Siluer. The Vsurer puts out a hundred pound to breede, and lets it run in a good pasture (thats to say, in the lands that are mortgag'd for it) till it grow great with Foale, and bring forth ten pound more. But the Politick Bankrupt playes the Alchimist, and hauing taken a hundred pound to multiply it, he keepes a puffing and a blowing, as if he would fetch the Philosophers stone out of it, yet melts your hundred pound so leng in his Crusibles, till at length he either melt it cleane away, or (at the least) makes him that lends it thinke good, if euery hundred bring him home fiue, with Principall and Interest.

You may behold now in this Perspectiue piece which I haue drawne before you, how deadly and dangerous an enemy to the State this Politick Bankruptisme hath bin, and still is: It hath bin long enough in the Citty, and for any thing I see, makes no great haste to get out. His triumphs haue bin great, his entertainement rich and magnificent. He purposes to lye heere as Lucifers Legiar: let him therefore alone in his lodging (in what part of the Citty soeuer it be) tossed and turmoyled with godlesse slumbers, and let vs take vp a standing neere some other Gate, to behold the Entrance of the Second Sinne: but before you go, looke vpon the Chariot that this First is drawne in, and take speciall note of all his Attendants.

The habit, the qualities and complexion of this Embassador sent from Hell, are set downe before. He rides in a Chariot drawne vpon three wheeles, that run fastest away, when they beare the greatest loades. The bewty of the Chariot is all in-layd work, cunningly and artificially wrought, but yet so strangely, and of so mony seuerall-fashiond pieces, (none like another) that a sound wit would mistrust they had bin stolne from sundry workemen. By this prowd Counterfet ran two Pages; on the left side Conscience, raggedly attirde, ill-fac'd, ill-coloured, and misshapen in body. On the right side runs Beggery, who if he out-liue him, goes to serue his children. Hipocrisy driues the

Chariot, hauing a couple of fat well-coloured and lusty Coach-horses to the eye, cald Couetousnes and Cosenage, but full of diseases, and rotten about the heart. Behind him follow a crowd of Trades-men, and Merchants, euery one of them holding either a Shop-booke, or an Obligation in his hand, their seruants, wiues and children strawing the way before him with curses, but he carelesly runnes ouer the one, and out-rides the other; at the tayle of whom (like the Pioners of an Army) march troopewise, and without any Drum struck vp, because the Leader can abide no noyse, a company of old expert Sarieants, bold Yeomen, hungry Baylifs, and other braue Martiall men, who because (like the Switzers) they are well payd, are still in Action, and oftentimes haue the enemy in execution; following the heeles of this Citty-Conqueror, so close, not for any loue they owe him, but only (as all those that follow great men do) to get mony by him. We will leaue them lying in Ambush, or holding their Courts of Gard, and take a muster of our next Regiment.

2. Lying.

Or,

The second dayes Triumph.

WHEN it came to the eares of the Sinfull
Synagogue, how the rich Iew of London,
(Barabbas Bankruptisme) their brother,
was receyued into the Citty, and what a
lusty Reueler he was become, the rest of the
same Progeny (being 6. in number) vowd to
ryde thither in their greatest State, and that
euery one should challenge to himselfe (if he
could enter) a seuerall day of Tryumph; for
so he might doe by their owne Customes.
Another therefore of the Broode, being presently aptly accoustred, and armed Cap-a-pe,
with all furniture fit for such an Inuader,
sets forward the very next morning, and
arriu'de at one of the Gates, before any
Porters eyes were vnglewd. To knocke, hee
thought it no policy, because such fellowes
are commonly most churlish, when they are
most intreated, and are key-cold in their

comming downe to Strangers, except they be brybed : to stay there with such a confusion of faces round about him, till light should betray him, might call his Arriuall, being strange and hidden, into question; besides, he durst not send any Spy he had, to listen what newes went amongst the people, and whether any preparation were made for him, or that they did expect his approche, because indeede there was not any one of the Damned Crewe that followed his tayle, whom he durst trust for a true word. He resolues therefore to make his entrance, not by the sword, but by some sleyght, what storme or fayre weather soeuer should happen : And for that purpose, taking asunder his Charriot, (for it stood altogether like a Germane clock, or an English Iack or Turne-spit, vpon skrewes and vices) he scatters his Troope vpon the fielde and bye-way, into small companies, as if they had bene Irish beggers ; till at last espying certayne Colliers with Carts most sinfully loaden, for the Citty, and behind them certayne light Country Horse-women ryding to the Markets, hee mingled his Footemen carelesly amongst these, and by this Stratagem of Coales, brauely thorow Moore-gate, got within the Walles, where marching not like a plodding Grasyer with his Droues before him, but like a Citty-Captayne, with a Company (as pert as Taylours at a wedding) close at his heeles, because nowe they knewe they were out of feare) hee musters together all the Hackneymen and Horse-coursers in and about Colman-streete.

No sooner had these Sonnes and Heyres vnto Horse-shooes, got him into their eyes, but they wept for ioy to behold him; yet in the ende, putting vp their teares into bottles of Hay, which they held vnder their armes, and wyping their slubberd cheekes with wispes of cleane Strawe (prouyded for the nonce) they harnessed the Grand Signiors Caroach, mounted his Cauallery vpon Curtals, and so sent him most pompously (like a new elected Dutch Burgomaster) into the Citty.

He was lookt vpon strangely by all whom he met, for at the first, few or none knew him, few followed him, few bid him welcome: But after hee had spent heere a very little peece of time, after it was voyc'd that Monsieur Mendax came to dwell amongst them, and had brought with him all sorts of politick falshood and lying, what a number of Men, Women and Children fell presently in loue with him! There was of euery Trade in the City, and of euery profession some, that instantly were dealers with him: For you must note, that in a State so multitudinous, where so many flocks of people must be fed, it is impossible to haue some Trades to stand, if they should not Lye.

How quickly after the Art of Lying was once publiquely profest, were false Weights and false Measures inuented! and they haue since done as much hurt to the inhabitants of Citties, as the inuention of Gunnes hath done to their walles: for though a Lye haue but short legs (like a Dwarfes) yet it goes farre in a little time, Et crescit eundo, and at last prooues a tall fellow: the reason is, that Truth had euer but one Father, but Lyes are a thousand mens Bastards, and are begotten euery where.

Looke vp then (Thou thy Countryes Darling,) and behold what a diuelish Inmate thou hast intertained. The Genealogy of Truth is well knowne, for she was borne in Heauen, and dwels in Heauen: Falshood then and Lying must of necessity come out of that hot Country of Hell, from the line of Diuels: for those two are as opposite, as day and darkenes. What an vngracious Generation wilt thou mingle with thine, if thou draw not this from thee: What a number of vnhappy and cursed children will be left vpon thy hand? for Lying is Father to Falshood, and Grandsire to Periury: Frawd (with two faces) is his Daughter, a very Monster: Treason (with haires like Snakes) is his kinseman; a very Fury! how art thou inclos'd with danger? The Lye first deceiues thee, and to shoote the deceit off cleanly, an oath (like an Arrow) is drawne to the head, and that hits the marke. If a Lye, after it is molded, be not smooth enough, there is no instrument to burnish it, but an oath: Swearing giues it cullor, and a bright complexion. So that Oathes are Crutches, vpon whych Lyes (like lame soldiers) go, and neede no other pasport. Little oathes are able to beare vp great lyes: but great Lyes are able to beate downe great Families: For oathes are wounds that a man stabs into himselfe, yea, they are burning words that consume those who kindle them.

What fooles then are thy Buyers and Sellers to be abused by such hell-hounds? Swearing and Forswearing put into their hands perhaps the gaines of a little Siluer, but like those pieces which Iudas receiued, they are their destruction. Welth so gotten, is like a tree set in the depth of winter, it prospers not.

But is it possible (Thou leader of so great a Kingdome) that heretofore so many bonfires of mens bodies should be made before thee in the good quarrell of Trueth? and that now thou shouldst take part with her enemy? Haue so many Triple-pointed darts of Treason bin shot at the heads of thy Princes, because they would not take Truth out of thy Temples, and art thou now in League with false Witches that would kill thee? Thou art no Traueler, the habit of Lying therefore will not become thee, cast it off.

He that giues a soldier the Lye, lookes to receiue the stab: but what danger does he run vpon, that giues a whole City the Lye? yet must I venture to giue it thee. Let me tell thee then, that Thou doest Lye with Pride, and though thou art not so gawdy, yet art thou more costly in attiring thy selfe than the Court, because Pride is the Queene of Sinnes, thou hast chosen her to be thy Concubine, and hast begotten many base Sonnes and Daughters vpon her body, as Vainglory, Curiosity, Disobedience, Opinion, Disdaine, &c. Pride, by thy Lying with her, is growne impudent: She is now a common Harlot, and euery one hath vse of her body. The Taylor calls her his Lemman, he hath often got her great with child of Phantasticallity and Fashions, who no sooner came into the world, but the fairest Wiues of thy Tennants snatcht them vp into their armes, layd them in their laps and to their brests, and after they had plaid with them their pleasure, into the country were those two children (of the Taylors) sent to be nurst vp, so that they liue sometimes there, but euer and anon with thee.

Thou doest likewise Lye with Vsury: how often hast thou bin found in bed with her! How often hath she bin openly disgraced at the Crosse for a Strumpet! yet still doest thou keepe her company, and art not ashamed of it, because you commit Sinne together, euen in those houses that haue paynted posts standing at the Gates. What vngodly brats and kindred hath she brought thee? for vpon Vsury hast thou begotten Extortion, (a strong, but an vnmannerly child,) Hardnes of heart, a very murderer, and Bad Conscience, who is so vnruly, that he seemes to be sent vnto thee, to be thy euerlasting paine. Then hath she Sonnes in law, and they are all Scriueners: those Scriueners haue base sonnes, and they are

all common Brokers; those Brokers likewise
send a number into the world, and they are
all Common Theeues.

All of these may easily giue Armes: for
they fetch their discent from hell, where are
as many Gentlemen, as in any one place, in
any kingdome.

Thou doost lye with sundrie others, and
committest strange whoredomes, which by
vse and boldnesse growe so common, that
they seeme to be no whoredomes at all,
Yet thine owne abhominations would not
appeare so vilely, but that thou makest thy
buildings a Brothelry to others: for thou
sufferest Religion to lye with Hipocrisie:
Charity to lye with Ostentation: Friendship
to lye with Hollow-heartednes: the Churle
to lye with Simony: Iustice to lye with
Bribery, and last of all, Conscience to lye
with euery one. So that now shee is full of
diseases: But thou knowest the medicine
for al these Feauers that shake thee: be
therfore to thy selfe thine owne Phisitian,
and by strong Pilles purge away this second
infection that is breeding vpon thee, before
it strike to the heart.

Falshood and Lying thus haue had their
day, and like Almanackes of the last yeare,
are now gon out: let vs follow them a step

or two farther to see how they ride, and then (if we can) leaue them, for I perceiue it growes late, because Candle-light (who is next to enter vpon the stage) is making himself ready to act his Comicall Scenes. The Chariot then that Lying is drawne in, is made al of whetstones; Wantonnes and euil custome are his Horses: a Foole is the Coachman that driues them: a couple of swearing Fencers sometimes leade the Horses by the reynes, and sometimes flourish before them to make roome. Worshipfully is this Lord of Limbo attended, for Knights themselues follow close at his heeles; Mary they are not Post and Poyre-Knightes but one of the Post. Amongst whose traine is shuffled in a company of scambling ignorant Petti-foggars, leane Knaues and hungrie, for they liue vpon nothing but the scraps of the Law, and heere and there (like a Prune in White-broth) is stucke a spruice but a meere prating vnpractised Lawyers Clarke all in blacke. At the tayle of all (when this goodly Pageant is passed by) follow a crowde of euerie trade some, amongst whome least we be smothered, and bee taken to bee of the same list, let vs strike downe my way.

Namque odi profanum Vulgus.

3. Candle-light.

Or,

The Nocturnall Tryumph.

O Candle-light! and art thou one of the Cursed Crew? hast thou bin set at the Table of Princes, and Nobelmen? haue all sortes of people doone reuerence vnto thee, and stood bare so soone as euer they haue seene thee? haue Theeues, Traytors, and Murderers been affraide to come in thy presence, because they knewe thee iust, and that thou wouldest discouer them? And art thou now a harborer of all kindes of Vices? nay, doost thou play the capitall Vice thy selfe?

Hast thou had so many learned Lectures read before thee, and is the light of thy Vnderstanding now cleane put out, and haue so many profound schollers profited by thee? hast thou doone such good to Vniuersities, beene soch a guide to the Lame, and seene the dooing of so many

44

good workes, yet doest thou now looke dimly, and with a dull eye vpon al Goodnes? What comfort haue sickmen taken (in weary and irkesome nights) but onely in thee? thou hast been their Phisition and Apothecary, and when the rellish of nothing could please them, the very shadow of thee hath beene to them a restoratiue Consolation. The Nurse hath stilled her wayward Infant, shewing it but to thee: What gladnes hast thou put into Mariners bosomes, when thou hast met them on the Sea? What Ioy into the faint and benighted Trauailer when he has met thee on the land? How many poore Handy-craftes men by Thee haue earned the best part of their liuing? And art thou now become a Companion for Drunkards, for leachers, and for prodigalles? Art thou turnd Reprobate? thou wilt burne for it in hell, And so odious is this thy Apostacy, and hiding thy self from the light of the truth, that thy death and going out of the world, euen they that loue thee best, wil tread thee vnder their feete: yea I that haue thus plaid the Herrald, and proclaimed thy good parts, wil now play the Cryer and cal thee into open count, to arraigne thee for thy misdemeanors.

Let the world therefore vnderstand, that

this Tallow-facde Gentleman (cald Candle-light) so soone as euer the Sunne was gon out of sight, and that darkenes like a thief out of a hedge crept vpon the earth, sweate till hee dropt agen, with bustling to come into the Cittie. For hauing no more but one onely eye (and that fierie red with drinking and sitting vp late) he was ashamed to be seene by day, knowing he should be laught to scorne, and hooted at. He makes his entrance therefore at Aldersgate of set purpose, for though the streete be faire and spatious, yet few lightes in mistie euenings, vsing there to thrust out their golden heads he thought that the aptest circle for him to be raised in, because there his Glittering would make greatest show.

What expectation was there of his com-ming? setting aside the bonfiers, there is not more triumphing on Midsommer night. No sooner was he aduaunced vp into the moste famous Streetes, but a number of shops for ioy beganne to shut in: Mercers rolde vp their silkes and Veluets: the Gold-smithes drew backe their Plate, and all the Citty lookt like a priuate Play-house, when the windowes are clapt downe, as if some Nocturnal, or dismall Tragedy were pre-sently to be acted before all the Trades-men.

But Caualiero Candle-light came for no such solemnitie : No he had other Crackers in hand to which hee watcht but his houre to giue fire. Scarce was his entrance blown abroad, but the Bankrupt, the Fellon, and all that owed any mony, and for feare of arrests, or Iustices warrants, had like so many Snayles kept their houses ouer their heads al the day before, began now to creep out of their shels, and to stalke vp and down the streets as vprightly, and with as proud a gate as if they meant to knock against the starres with the crownes of their heads.

The damask-coated Cittizen, that sat in his shop both forenoone and afternoone, and lookt more sowerly on his poore neighbors, then if he had drunke a quart of Vineger at a draught, sneakes out of his owne doores, and slips into a Tauerne, where either alone, or with some other that battles their money together, they so plye themselues with penny pots, which (like small-shot) goe off, powring into their fat paunches, that at length they haue not an eye to see withall, nor a good legge to stand vpon. In which pickle if anye of them happen to be iustled downe by a post (that in spite of them will take the wall) and so reeles them into the kennell, who takes them vp or leades them home? who has them to bed, and with a pillow smothes this stealing so of good liquor, but that brazen-face Candle-light? Nay more, hee intices their verie Prentices to make their desperate sallyes out, and quicke retyres in (contrarie to the Oath of their Indentures) which are seauen yeares a swearing, onely for their Pintes, and away.

Tush, this is nothing! yong shopkeepers that haue newly ventured vpon the pikes of marriage, who are euery houre shewing their wares to their Customers, plying their businesse harder all day then Vulcan does his Anuile, and seeme better husbands than Fidlers that scrape for a poore liuing both day and night, yet euen these if they can but get Candle-light, to sit vp all night with them in any house of Reckning (thats to say in a Tauerne) they fall roundly to play the London prize, and thats at three seuerall weapons, Drinking, Dauncing, and Dicing, Their wiues lying all that time in their beds sighing like widowes, which is lamentable: the giddie-braind husbands wasting the portions they had with them, which lost once, they are (like Maiden-heades) neuer recouerable. Or which is worse, this going a Bat-fowling a nights, beeing noted by some wise yong-man or other, that knowes how to handle such cases, the bush is beaten for them at home, whilest they catch the bird abroade, but what bird is it? the Woodcocke.

Neuer did any Cittie pocket vp such wrong at the hands of one, ouer whom she is so iealous, and so tender, that in Winter nights if he be but missing, and hide himselfe in the darke, I know not how many Beadles are sent vp and downe the streetes to crie him: yet you see, there is more cause she should send out to curse him For what Villanies are not abroad so long as Candlelight is stirring? The Seruing-man dare then walke with his wench: the Priuate Puncke (otherwise called one that boords in London) who like a Pigeon sits billing all day within doores, and feares to steppe ouer the thresholde, does then walke the round till midnight, after she hath beene swaggering amongst pottle pots and Vintners boyes. Nay, the sober Perpetuana suited Puritane, that dares not (so much as by Moone-light) come neere the Suburb-shadow of a house, where they set stewed Prunes befor you, raps as boldly at the hatch, when he knowes Candle-light is within, as if he were a new chosen Constable.

When al doores are lockt vp, when no eyes are open, when birds sit silent in bushes, and beasts lie sleeping vnder hedges, when no creature can be smelt to be vp but they that may be smelt euery night a streets length ere you come at them, euen then doth this Ignis fatuus (Candle-light) walke like a Fire-drake into sundrie corners. If you will not beleeue this, shoote but your eye through the Iron grates into the Cellers of Vintners, there you shall see him hold his necke in a Iin, made of a clift hoope-sticke, to throttle him from telling tales, whilest they most abhominably iumble together all the papisticall drinkes that are brought from beyond-sea : the poore wines are rackt and made to confesse anie thing : the Spanish and the French meeting both in the bottome of the Cellar, conspire together in their cups, to lay the Englishman (if he euer come into their company) vnder the boord.

To be short, such strange mad musick doe they play vpon their Sacke-buttes, that if Candle-light beeing ouer come with the steeme of newe sweete Wines, when they are at worke, shoulde not tell them tis time to goe to bedde, they would make all the Hogges-heads that vse to come to the house, to daunce the Cannaries till they reeld

againe. When the Grape-mongers and hee
are parted, hee walkes vp and downe the
streetes squiring olde Midwiues to anie
house, (verie secretly) where any Bastards
are to be brought into the worlde. From
them, (about the houre when Spirits walke,
and Cats goe a gossipping) hee visits the
Watch, where creeping into the Beadles
Cothouse (which standes betweene his
legges, that are lapt rounde about with
peeces of Rugge, as if he had newe strucke
of Shackles) and seeing the Watch-men
to nodde at him, hee hydes himselfe presently, (knowing the token) vnder the flappe
of a gowne, and teaches them (by instinct)
howe to steale nappes into their heades,
because hee sees all their Cloakes haue not
one good nappe vppon them: and vppon
his warrant snort they so lowde, that to
those Night-walkers (whose wittes are vp so
late) it serues as a Watch-worde to keepe
out of the reach of their browne Billes: by
which meanes they neuer come to aunswere
the matter before maister Constable, and the
Bench vppon which his men (that shoulde
watch) doe sitte: so that the Counters are
cheated of Prisoners, to the great dammage
of those that shoulde haue their mornings
draught out of the Garnish.

O Candle-light, Candle-light! to howe manie costly Sacke-possets, and reare Banquets hast thou beene inuited by Prentices and Kitchen-maidens? When the Bell-man for anger to spie (such a Purloyner of Cittizens goods) so many, hath bounced at the doore like a madde man, At which (as if Robin Good-fellow had beene coniur'd vp amongst them) the Wenches haue falne into the handes of the Greene-sicknesse, and the yong fellowes into colde Agues, with verie feare least their maister (like olde Ieronimo and Isabella his wife after him) starting out of his naked bed should come downe (with a Weapon in his hande) and this in his mouth: What out-cryes pull vs from our naked bedde? Who calles? &c. as the Players can tell you. O Candle-light, howe hast thou stuncke then, when they haue popt thee out of their companye: howe hast thou taken it in snuffe, when thou hast beene smelt out especially the maister of the house exclayming, that by day that deede of darknesse had not beene. One Vennie more with thee, and then I haue done.

How many lips haue beene worne out with kissing at the street doore, or in the entry (in a winking blind euening?) how many odde matches and vneuen mariages haue been made there betweene young Prentises and there maisters daughters, whilest thou (O Candle-light) hast stood watching at the staires heade, that none could come stealing downe by thee, but they must bee seene?

It appeares by these articles put in against thee, that thou art partly a Bawd to diuerse loose sinnes, and partly a Coozener: for if any in the Cittie haue badde wares lying deade vppon their handes, thou art better than Aqua vitæ to fetch life into them, and to sende them packing. Thou shalt therefore bee taken out of thy proude Chariot, and bee carted: yet first will wee see what workmanship, and what stuffe it is made of, to the intent that if it bee not daungerous for a Cittie to keepe anie Relique belonging to such a crooked Saint, It may bee hung vp as a monument to shewe with what dishonour thou wert driuen out of so noble a lodging, to deface whose buildings thou hast beene so enuious, that when thou hast beene left alone by any thing that woulde take fire, thou hast burnt to the ground many of her goodlyest houses.

Candle lights Coach is made all of Horne, shauen as thin as Changelinges are. It is drawne (with ease) by two Rats: the Coachman is a Chaundler, who so sweats with yeacking them, that he drops tallowe, and that feedes them as prouender: yet are the lashes that hee giues the squeaking Vermine, more deadly to them then al the Ratsbane in Bucklersburie. Painefulnesse and Studdy are his two Lackeyes and run by him: Darknesse, Conspiracy, Opportunitie, Stratagems and Feare, are his attendants: hee's sued vnto by Diggars in Mines, Grauers, Schollers, Mariners, Nurses, Drunkards, Vnthriftes and shrode Husbands: hee destroyes that which feedes him, and therefore Ingratitude comes behinde all this, driuing them before her. The next Diuel that is to be commaunded vp, is a very lazie one, and will be long in rising: let vs therefore vnbinde this, and fall to other Charmes.

4. Sloth

Or

The fourth dayes Tryumph.

MAN (doubtlesse) was not created to bee
an idle fellow, for then he should bee Gods
Vagabond: he was made for other purpose
then to be euer eating as swine: euer sleeping as Dormise: euer dumb as fishes in the
Sea, or euer prating to no purpose, as
birdes of the ayre: he was not set in this
Vniuersall Orchard to stand still as a
Tree, and so to bee cut downe, but to be
cut downe if he should stand still. And to
haue him remember this, he carries certaine Watches with Larums about him, that
are euer striking: for all the Enginous
Wheeles of the Soule are continually going:
though the body lye neuer so fast bownde
in Slumbers, the imagination runnes too
and fro, the phantasie flyes round about,
the vitall Spirits walke vp and downe,
yea the very pulses shew actiuitie, and

55

their hammers are still beating, so that euen in his very dreames it is whispered in his eare that hee must bee dooing something.

If hee had not these prompters at his elbowe, yet euerie member of his body (if it could speake would chide him) if they were put to no vse, considering what noble workmanship is bestowed vpon them. For man no sooner gets vpon his legges, but they are made so that either hee may run or goe: when he is weary, they can giue him ease by standing still, if he will not stand, the Knees serue like Hindges to bow vp and downe, and to let him kneele. His armes haue artificiall cordes and stringes, which shorten or flye out to their length at pleasure: They winde about the bodye like a siluer Girdle, and being held out before, are weapons to defend it: at the end of the armes, are two beautiful Mathematicall Instruments, with fiue seuerall motions in each of them, and thirtie other mouing Engines, by which they stirre both. His head likewise standes vppon three Skrewes, the one is directly forward to teach him Prouidence, the other two are on eather side one, to arme him with Circumspection: How busie are both the eyes, to keepe danger from him euerie way.

But admit hee had none of these Wonderfull Volumes to reade ouer, yet hee sees the clowdes alwaies working: the waters euer labouring: the earth continuallye bringing foorth: he sees the Sunne haue a hye colour with taking paines for the day. The Moone pale and sickly, with sitting vp for the night: the Stars mustring their armyes together to guard the Moone. All of them, and all that is in the world, seruing as Schoolemaisters, and the world it selfe as an Academ to bring vp man in knowledge, and to put him still into action.

How then dares this nastie, and loathsome sin of Sloth venture into a Citie amongst so many people? who doth he hope wil giue him entertainment? what lodging (thinks he) can be taine vp, where he and his heauy-headed company may take their afternoones nap soundly? for in euery street, carts and Coaches make such a thundring as if the world ranne vpon wheeles: at euerie corner, men, women, and children meete in such shoales, that postes are sette vp of purpose to strengthen the houses, least with iustling one another they should shoulder them downe. Besides, hammers are beating in one place, Tubs hooping in another, Pots clincking in a

third, water-tankards running at tilt in a
fourth : heere are Porters sweating vnder
burdens, there Marchants-men bearing bags
of money, Chapmen (as if they were at
Leape-frog) skippe out of one shop into
another : Tradesmen (as if they were
dauncing Galliards) are lusty at legges
and neuer stand still: all are as busie as
countrie Atturneyes at an Assises : how
then can Idlenes thinke to inhabit heere?

Yet the Worshipfull Sir, (that leades a
Gentlemans life, and dooth nothing) though
he comes but slowly on (as if hee trodde a
French March) yet hee comes and with a
great trayne at his tayle, as if the countrie
had brought vp some Fellon to one of our
Gayles, So is he conuaide by nine or tenne
drowsie Malt-men, that lye nodding ouer
their Sackes, and euen a moste sleepie
and still Triumph begins his entrance at
Bishopsgate.

An armie of substantiall Housholders
(moste of them liuing by the hardnesse of
the hand) came in Battaile array, with
spred Banners, bearing the Armes of their
seuerall occupations to meete this Cowardly
Generall and to beate him backe. But hee
sommoning a parlee, hammered out such
a strong Oration in praise of Ease, that

they all strucke vp their Drums, flung vp their Round-Cappes, (and as if it had beene another William the Conqueror came marching in with him) and lodged him in the quietest streete in the Cittie, for so his Lazinesse requested.

Hee then presently gaue licenses to all the Vintners, to keepe open house, and to emptye their Hogsheades to all commers, who did so, dying their grates into a drunkards blush (to make them knowne from the Grates of a prison) least customers should reele away from them, and hanging out new bushes, that if men at their going out, could not see the signe, yet they might not loose themselues in the bush. He likewise gaue order that dicing-houses, and bowling alleyes should be erected, wherupon a number of poore handy-crafts-men, that before wrought night and day, made stocks to themselues of ten groates, and crowns a peece, and what by Betting, Lurches, Rubbers and such tricks, they neuer tooke care for a good daies worke afterwards. For as Letchery is patron of al your Suburb Colledges, and sets vp Vaulting-houses, and Daunsing-Schooles: and as Drunkennesse when it least can stand, does best hold vp Alehouses, So Sloth is a founder of the Almeshouses first mentioned, and is a good Benefactor to these last.

The Players prayed for his comming, they lost nothing by it, the comming in of tenne Embassadors was neuer so sweete to them, as this our sinne was: their houses smoakt euerye after noone with Stinkards, who were so glewed together in crowdes with the Steames of strong breath, that when they came foorth, their faces lookt as if they had beene perboylde: And his Comicall Tearme-time they hoped for, at the least all the summer, because tis giuen out that Sloth himselfe will come, and sit in the two-pennie galleries amongst the Gentlemen, and see their Knaueries and their pastimes.

But alas! if these were the sorest diseases (Thou noblest City of the now-noblest Nation) that Idlenes does infect thee with: thou hast Phisick sufficient in thy selfe, to purge thy bodie of them. No, no, hee is not slothfull, that is onelye lazie, that onelye wastes his good houres, and his Siluer in Luxury, and licentious ease, or that onely (like a standing water) does nothing, but gather corruption: no, hee is the true Slothfull man that does no good. And how many would crie Guilty vnto

thee, if this were there Inditement? Thy
Maiestrates (that when they see thee most
in danger) put vp the swordes that Iustice
hath guided, to their loynes, and flie into
the countrie, leauing thee destitute of their
Counsell, they would crie guilty, they are
slothfull.

Thy Phisitions, that fearing to die by
that which they liue, (sicknes) doe most
vnkindely leaue thee when thou art ready
to lye vpon thy death bed, They are sloth-
ful, They would crie Guilty. Thy great
men, and such as haue been thy Rulers,
that being taken out of poore Cradles, and
nursed vp by thee, haue fild their Cofers
with golde, and their names with honour,
yet afterwards growing weary of thee, (like
Mules hauing suckt their dammes) most
ingratefully haue they stolne from thee,
spending those blessings which were thine,
vpon those that no way deserue them, Are
not These Slothfull? They would crie
guiltye. There is yet one more, whome I
would not heare to Cry Guilty, because (of
all others) I would not haue them slothfull.
O you that speake the language of Angels,
and should indeed be Angels amongst vs,
you that haue offices aboue those of Kinges,
that haue warrant to commaund Princes,

and controle them, if they do amisse: you that are Stewards ouer the Kings house of heauen, and lye heere as Embassadors about the greatest State-matters in the world: what a dishonour were it to your places, if it should bee knowne that you are Sloath-full? you are sworne labourers, to worke in a Vineyard, which if you dresse not carefully, if you cut it not artificially, if you vnderprop it not wisely when you see it laden, if you gather not the fruites in it, when they bee ripe, but suffer them to drop downe, and bee eaten vp by Swine. O what a deere account are you to make him that must giue you your hire? you are the Beames of the Sun that must ripen the grapes of the Vine, and if you shine not cleerely, he will eclipse you for euer: your tongues are the instruments that must cut off rancke and idle Sprigs, to make the bearing-braunches to spred, and vnlesse you keep them sharpe and be euer pruning with them, he will cast you by, and you shall be eaten vp with rust. The Church is a garden and you must weede it: it is a Fountaine, and you must keepe it cleere: it is her Husbands Jewell, and you must pollish it: it is his best belooued, and you must keepe her chast.

Many Merchants hath this Cittie to her Sonnes, of al which you are the most noble, you trafficke onely for mens Soules, sending them to the Land of Promise, and to the heauenly Ierusalem, and receiuing from thence (in Exchange) the richest Commoditie in the world, your owne saluation. O therefore bee not you Slothfull: for if being chosen Pilots, you Sleepe, and so sticke vpon Rockes, you hazard your owne shipwracke more then theirs that venture with you.

What a number of Colours are here grounded, to paint out Sloth in his vglines, and to make him loathed, whilst he (yawning, and his Chin knocking nods into his brest) regardes not the whips of the moste crabbish Satyristes. Let vs therfore looke vpon his Horse-litter that hee rides in, and so leaue him.

A couple of vnshodde Asses carry it betweene them, it is all sluttishly ouergrowne with Mosse on the out-side, and on the inside quilted through out with downe pillowes: Sleepe and Plenty leade the Fore-Asse; a pursie double chind Læna, riding by on a Sumpter-horse with prouander at his mouth, and she is the Litter-Driuer: shee keepes two Pages, and those are an

Irish Beggar on the one side, and One that sayes he has been a Soldier on the other side. His attendants are Sicknes, Want, Ignorance, Infamy, Bondage, Palenes, Blockishnes, and Carelesnes. The Retayners that wear his cloth are Anglers, Dumb Ministers, Players, Exchange-Wenches, Gamsters, Panders, Whores and Fidlers.

Apishnesse:

Or

The fift dayes Triumph

SLOTH was not so slow in his march,
when hee entred the Citie, but Apishnesse
(that was to take his turne next) was as
quick. Do you not know him? It cannot
be read in any Chronicle, that he was euer
with Henrie the eight at Bulloigne or at the
winning of Turwin and Turnay: for (not
to belie the sweete Gentleman,) he was
neither in the shell then, no nor then when
Paules-steeple and the Weathercocke were
on fire; by which markes (without looking
in his mouth) you may safely sweare, that
hees but yong, for hees a feirse, dapper
fellow, more light headed then a Musitian:
as phantastically attyred as a Court Ieaster:
wanton in discourse: lasciuious in behauiour: iocond in good companie: nice
in his trencher, and yet he feedes verie
hungerly on scraps of songs: he drinkes

in a Glasse well, but vilely in a deepe French-bowle : yet much about the yeare when Monsieur came in, was hee begotten, betweene a French Tayler, and an English Court-Seamster. This Signior Ioculento (as the diuell would haue it) comes prawncing in at Cripplegate, and he may well doe it, for indeede all the parts hee playes are but con'd speeches stolne from others, whose voices and actions hee counterfeites : but so lamely, that all the Cripples in tenne Spittle-houses, shewe not more halting. The Grauer Browes were bent against him, and by the awfull Charms of Reuerend Authoritie, would haue sent him downe from whence he came, for they knew howe smooth soeuer his lookes were, there was a diuell in his bosome : But hee hauing the stronger faction on his side, set them in a Mutenie, Sæuitque animis ignobile vulgus, the manie headed Monster fought as it had beene against Saint George, won the gate, and then with showtes was the Gaueston of the Time, brought in. But who brought him in? None but richmens sonnes that were left well, and had more money giuen by will, then they had wit how to bestow it : none but Prentises almost out of their yeers, and all the Tailors, Haberdashers, and Embroderers that could be got for loue or money, for these were prest secretly to the seruice, by the yong and wanton dames of the Citie, because they would not be seene to shewe their loue to him themselues.

Man is Gods Ape, and an Ape is Zani to a man, doing ouer those trickes (especially if they be knauish) which hee sees done before him: so that Apishnesse is nothing but counterfetting or imitation: and this flower when it first came into the Citie, had a prettie scent, and a delightfull colour, hath bene let to run so high, that it is now seeded, and where it fals there rises vp a stinking weede.

For as man is Gods Ape, striuing to make artificiall flowers, birdes, &c. like to the naturall: So for the same reason are women, Mens Shee Apes, for they will not bee behind them the bredth of a Taylors yard (which is nothing to speake of) in anie new-fangled vpstart fashion. If men get vp French standing collers, women will haue the French standing coller too: if Dublets with little thick skirts, (so short that none are able to sit vpon them,) womens fore-parts are thick skirted too: by surfetting vpon which kinde of phantasticall Apishnesse in a short time, they fall into the disease of pride: Pride is infectious, and breedes prodigalitie: Prodigalitie after it has runne a little, closes vp and festers, and then turns to Beggerie. Wittie was that Painter therefore, that when hee had limned one of euery Nation in their proper attyres, and beeing at his wittes endes howe to drawe an Englishman: At the last (to giue him a quippe for his follie in apparell) drewe him starke naked, with Sheeres in his hand, and cloth on his arme, because none could cut out his fashions but himselfe.

For an English-mans suite is like a traitors bodie that hath beene hanged, drawne, and quartered, and is set vp in seuerall places: his Codpeece is in Denmarke, the collor of his Duble, and the belly in France: the wing and narrowe sleeue in Italy: the short waste hangs ouer a Dutch Botchers stall in Vtrich: his huge sloppes speakes Spanish: Polonia giues him the Bootes: the blocke for his heade alters faster then the Feltmaker can fitte him, and thereupon we are called in scorne Blockheades. And thus we that mocke euerie Nation, for keeping one fashion, yet steale patches from euerie one of them, to peece out our pride, are now laughing-stocks to them, because their cut so scuruily becomes vs:

This sinne of Apishnesse, whether it bee in apparell, or in diet, is not of such long life as his fellowes, and for seeing none but women and fooles keepe him companie, the one wil be ashamed of him when they begin to haue wrinckles, the other when they feele their purses light. The Magistrate, the wealthy commoner, and the auncient Cittizen, disdaine to come neare him: wee were best therefore, take note of such things as are aboute him, least on a suddaine hee slip out of sight.

Apishnesse rides in a Chariot made of nothing but cages, in which are all the strangest out-landish Birds that can be gotten: the Cages are stucke full of Parats feathers: the Coach-man is an Italian Mownti-banck who driues a Fawne and a Lambe, for they drawe this Gew-gaw in Winter, when such beasts are rarest to be had: In Sommer, it goes alone by the motion of wheeles: two Pages in light coloured suites, embrodered full of Butter-flies, with wings that flutter vp with the winde, run by him, the one being a dauncing boy the other a Tumbler: His attendants

69

are Folly, Laughter, Inconstancie, Riot, Nicenesse, and Vainglorie : when his Court remoues, hee is folowed by Tobacconists, Shittlecock - makers, Feathermakers, Cob-web-lawne-weauers, Perfumers, young, Countrie Gentlemen, and Fooles, In whose Ship whilest they all are sayling, let vs obserue what other abuses the Verdimotes Inquest doe present on the lande, albeit they bee neuer reformed, till a second Chaos is to bee refined. In the meane time, In noua fert Animus.

Shauing:

Or

The sixt dayes Triumph.

HOW? Shauing! Me thinkes Barbers
should crie to their Customers winck hard
and come running out of their shoppes into
the open streetes, throwing all their Suddes
out of their learned Latin Basons into my
face for presuming to name the Mysterie of
Shauing in so villanous a companie as
these seuen are. Is that Trade (say they)
that for so many yeares hath beene held vp
by so many heades, and has out-bearded
the stowtest in England to their faces, Is
that Trade, that because it is euermore
Trimming the Citie, hath beene for many
yeers past made vp into a Societie, and
hane their Guild, and their Priuiledges
with as much freedome as the best, must
that nowe bee counted a sinne (nay and
one of the Deadly sinnes) of the Cittie?
No, no, be not angry with me, (O you that

bandie away none but sweete washing
Balles, and cast none other then Rose-
waters for any mans pleasure) for there is
Shauing within the walles of this Great
Metropolis, which you neuer dreamed of:
A shauing that takes not only away the
rebellious haires, but brings the flesh with
it too: and if that cannot suffice, the very
bones must follow. If therfore you, and
Fiue companies greater then yours, should
chuse a Colonel, to lead you against this
mightie Tamburlaine, you are too weake to
make him Retire, and if you should come
to a battell, you would loose the day.

For behold what Troopes forsake the
Standard of the Citie, and flie to him:
neither are they base and common souldiers,
but euen those that haue borne armes a
long time. Be silent therfore, and be
patient: and since there is no remedie but
that (this combatant that is so cunning at
the sharp) wil come in, mark in what
triumphant and proud manner, he is
marshalled through Newgate: At which
Bulwarke (and none other) did he (in
policy) desire to shew himself. First, because he knew if the Citie should play
with him as they did with Wiat, Newgate
held a number, that though they were false

to all the world, would be true to him. Couragiously therfore does he enter: All of them that had once serued vnder his colors (and were now to suffer for the Truth, which they had abused) leaping vp to the Iron lattaces, to beholde their General, and making such a ratling with shaking their chaines for ioy, as if Cerberus had bin come from hell to liue and die amongst them. Shauing is now lodged in the heart of the Citie, but by whom? and at whose charges? Mary at a common purse, to which many are tributaries, and therfore no maruell if he be feasted royally. The first that paid their mony towards it, are cruel and couetous Land-lords, who for the building vp of a Chimny, which stands them not aboue 30. s. and for whiting the wals of a tenement, which is scarce worth the daubing, raise the rent presently (as if it were new put into the Subsidy book) assessing it at 3. li. a yeer more then euer it went for before: filthy wide-mouthd bandogs they are, that for a quarters rent will pull out their ministers throte, if he were their tenant: And (though it turn to the vtter vndoing of a man) being rubd with quicksiluer, which they loue because they haue mangy consciences, they will let to a drunken Flemming a house ouer his own country-man head, thinking hees safe enough from the thunderbolts of their wiues and children, and from curses, and the very vengeance of heauen, if he get by the bargaine, but so many Angels as will couer the crowne of his head.

The next that laide downe his share, was no Sharer among the Players, but a shauer of yong Gentlemen, before euer a haire dare peepe out of their chinnes: and these are Vsurers: who for a little money, and a greate deal of trash: (as Fire-shouels, browne-paper, motley cloake-bags, &c.) bring yong Nouices into a fooles Paradice till they haue sealed the Morgage of their landes, and then like Pedlers, goe they (or some Familiar spirit for them raizde by the Vsurer) vp and downe to cry Commodities) which scarce yeeld the third part of the sum for which they take them vp.

There are likewise other Barbers, who are so well customed, that they shaue a whole Citie sometymes in three dayes, and they doe it (as Bankes his horse did his tricks) onely by the eye, and the eare: For if they either see no Magistrate comming towardes them, (as being called back by the Common-weale for more serious imployments) or doe but heare that hee lyes sicke, vpon whom the health of a Cittie is put in hazard : they presently (like Prentises vpon Shoue-tuesday) take the lawe into their owne handes, and doe what they list. And this Legion consists of Market-folkes, Bakers, Brewers, all that weigh their Consciences in Scales. And lastly, of the two degrees of Colliers, viz. those of Char-coles, and those of New-castle. Then haue you the Shauing of Fatherlesse children, and of widowes, and thats done by Executors. The shauing of poore Clients especially by the Atturneyes Clearkes of your Courts, and thats done by writing their Billes of costs vpon Cheuerell. The Shauing of prisoners by extortion, first, taken by their keepers, for a prison is builded on such ranke and fertil ground, that if poore wretches sow it with hand-fulles of small debts when they come in, if they lie there but a while to see the comming vp of them : the charges of the house will bee treble the demaund of the Creditor. Then haue you Brokers that shaue poor men by most iewish interest : marry the diuils trimme them so soone as they haue washed others. I wil not tell how Vintners shaue their Guestes with a little peece of Paper

not aboue three fingers broade; for their
roomes are like Barbars Chaires: Men
come into them willingly to bee Shauen.
Onely (which is worst) bee it knowne to
thee (O thou Queene of Cities) thy Inhabitants Shaue their Consciences so close,
that in the ende they growe balde, and
bring foorth no goodnesse.

Wee haue beene quicke (you see) in
Trimming this Cutter of Queene Hith, because tis his propertie to handle others
so, let vs bee as nymble in praysing his
Household-stuffe: The best part of which
is his Chariot, richly adorned, It is drawen
by foure beasts: the 2. formost are a Wolfe
(which will eate till he be readie to burst)
and hee is Coach-fellow to a she-Beare,
who is cruell euen to women great with
childe: behinde them are a couple of
Blood-houndes: the Coach-man is an In-
former. Two Pettifoggers that haue beene
turned ouer the barre, are his Lackies:
his Houshold seruants are Wit (who is
his Steward) Audacitie: Shifting: Inexora-
bilitie: and Disquietnesse of mind: The
Meanie are (besides some persons before
named) skeldring soldiers, and begging
schollers.

Crueltie;

Or

The seuenth and last dayes Triumph.

WHAT a weeke of sinfull Reueling hath heere bin with these six proud Lords of Misrule? to which of your Hundred parishes (O you citizens) haue not some one of these (if not all) remoued their Courts, and feasted you with them? your Percullises are not strong inough to keepe them out by day your Watchmen are too sleepy to spie their stealing in by night. There is yet another to enter, as great in power as his fellowes, as subtill, as full of mischiefe : If I shoulde name him to you, you would laugh mee to scorne, because you cannot bee perswaded that such a one should euer bee suffered to liue within the freedome: yet if I name him not to you, you may in time, by him (as by the rest) bee vndone.   It is Crueltie, O strange!

mee thinkes London should start vp out of her sollid foundation, and in anger bee ready to fall vppon him, and grinde him to dust that durst say, shee is possest with such a deuill. Cruelty! the verie sound of it shewes that it is no English word: it is a Fury sent out of hel, not to inhabit within such beautifull walles, but amongst Turkes and Tartars. The other sixe Monsters transforme themselues into Amiable shapes, and set golden, inticing Charmes to winne men to their Circæan loue, they haue Angelical faces to allure, and bewitching tongues to inchaunt: But Cruelty is a hag, horred in forme, terrible in voice, formidable in threates, A tyrant in his very lookes, and a murderer in all his actions.

How then commeth it to passe that heere he seekes entertainment? For what Cittie in the world, does more drie vp the teares of the Widdowe, and giues more warmth to the fatherlesse then this ancient and reuerend Grandam of Citties? Where hath the Orphan (that is to receiue great portions) lesse cause to mourne the losse of Parents? He findes foure and twentie graue Senators to bee his Fathers instead of one: the Cittie it selfe to bee his Mother:

her Officers to bee his Seruants, who see that hee want nothing: her lawes to suffer none to doe him wrong: and though he be neuer so simple in wit, or so tender in yeares, shee lookes as warily to that welth which is left him, as to the Apple of her owne eye. Where haue the Leaper and the Lunatick Surgery, and Phisicke so good cheape as heere? their payment is onely thankes: large Hospitalls are erected (of purpose to make them lodgings) and the rent is most easie, onely their prayers: yet for all this, that Charitie hath her Armes full of children, and that tender-brested Compassion is still in one street or other dooing good workes: off from the Hindges are one of the 7. Gates readie to bee lifted, to make roome for this Giant: the Whiflers of your inferior and Chiefe companies cleere the wayes before him, men of all trades with shoutes and acclamations followed in thronges behinde him, yea euen the siluer-bearded, and seuearest lookt cittizens haue giuen him welcomes in their Parlors.

There are in Lond. and within the buildings, that round about touch her sides, and stand within her reach, Thirteene strong houses of sorrow, where the prisoner hath his heart wasting away sometimes a whole prentiship of yeres in cares. They are most of them built of Freestone, but none are free within them: cold are their imbracements: vnwholsom is their cheare: dispaireful their lodgings, vncomfortable their societies, miserable their inhabitants: O what a deale of wretchednes can make shift to lye in a little roome! if those 13 houses were built al together, how rich wold Griefe be, hauing such large inclosures? Doth cruelty challenge a freemans roome in the City because of these places? no, the politicke body of the Republike wold be infected, if such houses as these were not maintained, to keep vp those that are vnsound. Claimes he then an inheritance here, because you haue whipping postes in your streetes for the Vagabond? the Stocks and the cage for the vnruely beggar? or because you haue Carts for the Bawde and the Harlot, and Beadles for the Lecher? neither. Or is it because so many monthly Sessions are held? so many men, women and Children cald to a reconing at the Bar of death for their liues? and so many lamentable hempen Tragedies acted at Tiburne? nor for this: Iustice should haue wrong, to haue it so reported. No (you Inhabitants of this little world of people) Crueltie is a large Tree and you all stand vnder it: you are cruel in compelling your children (for wealth) to goe into loathed beds, for therby Against forced Mariages. you make them bond-slaues: what plough-man is so foolish to yoake young heefars and old bullocks together? yet such is your husbandry. In fitting your Coaches with horses, you are very curious to haue them (so neere as you can), both of a colour, both of a height, of an age, of proportion, and will you bee carelesse in coupling your Children? he into whose bosome threescore winters haue thrust their frozen fingars, if hee be rich (though his breath bee rancker then a Muck-hill, his bodye more drye than Mummi, and his minde more lame than Ignorance it selfe) shall haue offered vnto him (but it is offered as a sacrifice) the tender bossome of a Virgin, vpon whose fore-head was neuer written sixteene yeares: if she refuse this liuing death (for lesse than a death it cannot be vnto her) She is threatned to bee left an out-cast, cursd for disobedience, raild at daily, and reuylde howerlye: to saue herselfe from which basenes, She desprately runnes into a bondage, and goes to Church to be married, as if she went to be buried. But what glorye atcheiue you in these conquests? you doe wrong to Time, inforcing May to embrace December: you dishonour Age, in bringing it into scorne for insufficiency, into a loathing for dotage, into all mens laughter for iealousie. You made your Daughters looke wrinckled with sorrowes, before they be olde, and your sonnes by riot, to be beggars in midst of their youth. Hence comes it, that murders are often contriued, and as often acted: our countrie is woful in fresh examples: Hence comes it, that the Courtiers giues you an open scoffe, the clown a secret mock, the Cittizen that dwels at your threshald, a ieery frump: Hence it is that if you goe by water in the calmest day, you are driuen by some fatall storme into that vnlucky and dangerous hauen betweene Greenewich and London. You haue another cruelty in keeping men in prison so long, til sicknes and death deal mildely with them, and (in despite of al tyranny) baile them out of all executions. When you see a poore wretch that to keep life in a loathed body hath not a house left to couer his head from

Against cruell Creditors.

82

the tempestes, nor a bed (but the common bedde which our Mother the earth allowes him) for his cares to sleepe vppon, when you haue (by keeping or locking him vp,) robd him of all meanes to get, what seeke you to haue him loose but his life? The miserable prisoner is ready to famish, yet that cannot mooue you, the more miserable wife is readye to runne mad with dispaire, yet that cannot melt you: the moste of all miserable, his Children lye crying at your dores, yet nothing can awaken in you compassion: if his debts be heauie, the greater and more glorious is your pitty to worke his freedome, if they be light, the sharper is the Vengeance that will be heaped vpon your heades for your hardnes of heart. Wee are moste like to God that made vs, when wee shew loue one to another, and doe moste looke like the Diuell that would destroy vs, when wee are one anothers tormenters. If any haue so much flint growing about his bosome, that he will needes make Dice of mens bones, I would there were a lawe to compell him to make drinking bowles of their Sculs too: and that euerie miserable debter that so dyes, might be buried at his Creditors doore, that when hee strides ouer him he might thinke he still rises vp (like the Ghost in Ieronimo) crying Reuenge.

Crueltie hath yet another part to play, it is acted (like the old Morralls Against vnconsionable Maisters. at Maningtree) by Trades-men, marrye seuerall companies in the Cittie haue it in study, and they are neuer perfect in it, till the end of seauen yeares at least, at which time, they come off with it roundly. And this it is: When your seruants haue made themselues bondmen to inioy your fruitefull hand-maides, thats to say, to haue an honest and thriuing Art to liue by: when they haue fared hardly with you by Indenture, and like your Beasts which carry you haue patiently borne al labours, and all wrongs you could lay vpon them.

When you haue gathered the blossomes of their youth, and reaped the fruites of their strength, And that you can no longer (for shame) hold them in Captiuitie, but that by the lawes of your Country and of conscience you must vndoe their fetters, Then, euen then doe you hang moste weightes at their heeles, to make them sincke downe for euer: when you are bound to send them into the world to liue, you send them into the world to beg: they

seru'd you seuen yeeres to pick vp a poore
liuing, and therein you are iust, for you
will be sure it shall be a poore liuing
indeede they shall pick vp : for what do
the rich cubs? like foxes they lay their
heads together in conspiracy, burying their
leaden consciences vnder the earth, to the
intent that all waters that are wholesome
in taste, and haue the sweetnes of gaine
in going downe, may be drawne through
them only, being the great pipes of their
Company, because they see 'tis the custome
of the Citty, to haue all waters that come
thither, conueyed by such large vessels,
and they will not breake the customes of
the Citty. When they haue the fulnesse
of welth to the brim, that it runs ouer,
they scarce will suffer their poore Seruant
to take that which runs at waste, nor to
gather vp the wind-fals, when all the great
trees, as if they grew in the garden of the
Hesperides, are laden with golden apples:
no, they would not haue them gleane the
scattered eares of corne, though they themselues cary away the full sheafes ; as if
Trades that were ordaind to be Com-
munities, had lost their first priuiledges,
and were now turnd to Monopolyes. But
remember (ô you Rich men) that your

Seruants are your adopted Children, they are naturalized into your bloud, and if you hurt theirs, you are guilty of letting out your owne, than which, what Cruelty can be greater?

What Gallenist or Paracelsian in the world, by all his water-casting, and minerall extractions, would iudge, that this fairest-fac'de daughter of Brute, (and good daughter to King Lud, who gaue her her name) should haue so much corruption in her body? vnlesse (that beeing now two thousand and seuen hundred yeeres old) extreme age should fill her full of diseases! Who durst not haue sworne for her, that of all loathsome sinnes that euer bred within her, she had neuer toucht the sinne of cruelty? It had wont to be a Spanish Sicknes, and hang long (incurably) vpon the body of their Inquisition; or else a French disease, running all ouer that Kingdome in a Massacre; but that it had infected the English, especially the people of this now once-againe New-reard-Troy, it was beyond beliefe. But is she cleerely purg'd of it by those pills that haue before bin giuen her? Is she now sound? Are there no dregs of this thick and pestilenciall poyson, eating

still through her bowels? Yes: the vgliest
Serpent hath not vncurld himselfe. She
hath sharper and more black inuenomed
stings within her, than yet haue bin shot
forth.

There is a Cruelty within thee (faire
Troynouant) worse and more Against want
barbarous then all the rest, be- of places for Buriall in
cause it is halfe against thy owne extremity of sicknes.
selfe, and halfe against thy Dead
Sonnes and Daughters. Against thy dead
children wert thou cruell in that dreadfull,
horrid, and Tragicall yeere, when 30000 of
them (struck with plagues from 1602.
heauen) dropt downe in winding-
sheetes at thy feet. Thou didst then take
away all Ceremonies due vnto them, and
haledst them rudely to their last beds (like
drunkards) without the dead mans musick
(his Bell.) Alack, this was nothing: but
thou tumbledst them into their euerlasting
lodgings (ten in one heape, and twenty in
another) as if all the roomes vpon earth
had bin full. The gallant and the begger
lay together; the scholler and the carter in
one bed: the husband saw his wife, and
his deadly enemy whom he hated, within
a paire of sheetes. Sad and vnsemely are
such Funeralls: So felons that are cut

downe from the tree of shame and dishonor, are couered in the earth: So souldiers, after a mercilesse battaile, receiue vnhansome buriall. But suppose the Pestiferous Deluge should againe drowne this little world of thine, and that thou must be compeld to breake open those caues of horror and gastlinesse, to hide more of thy dead houshold in them, what rotten stenches, and contagious damps would strike vp into thy nosthrils? thou couldst not lift vp thy head into the aire, for that (with her condensed sinnes) would stifle thee; thou couldst not diue into the waters, for that they being teinted by the ayre, would poison thee. Art thou now not cruell against thy selfe, in not prouiding (before the land-waters of Affliction come downe againe vpon thee) more and more conuenient Cabins to lay those in, that are to goe into such farre countries, who neuer looke to come back againe? If thou shouldst deny it, the Graues when they open, will be witnesses against thee.

Nay, thou hast yet Another Cruelty gnawing in thy bosome; for what hope is there that thou shouldst haue pitty ouer others, when thou art vnmercifull to thy self! Looke

Against want of prouision for those that dye in the fields.

88

ouer thy walls into thy Orchards and Gardens, and thou shalt see thy seruants and apprentises sent out cunningly by their Masters at noone day vpon deadly errands, when they perceiue that the Armed Man hath struck them, yea euen when they see they haue tokens deliuered them from heauen to hasten thither, then send they them forth to walke vpon their graues, and to gather the flowers themselues that shall stick their own Herse. And this thy Inhabitants do, because they are loth and ashamed to haue a writing ouer their dores, to tell that God hath bin there, they had rather all their enemies in the world should put them to trouble, then that he should visit them.

Looke againe ouer the walls into thy Fields, and thou shalt heare poore and forsaken wretches lye groaning in ditches, and trauailing to seeke out Death vpon thy common hye wayes. Hauing found him, he there throwes downe their infected carcases, towards which, all that passe by, looke, but (till common shame, and common necessity compell) none step in to giue them buriall. Thou setst vp posts to whip them when they are aliue: Set vp an Hospitall to comfort them being sick, or purchase ground for them to dwell in when they be well, and that is, when they be dead.

Is it not now hye time to sound a Retreate, after so terrible a battaile fought betweene the seuen Electors of the Low Infernall Countryes, and one little Citty? What armyes come marching along with them? What bloudy cullors do they spread? What Artillery do they mount to batter the walls? How valiant are their seuen Generalls? How expert? How full of fortune to conquer? Yet nothing sooner ouerthrowes them, than to bid them battaile first, and to giue them defiance.

Who can denye now, but that Sinne (like the seuen-headed Nylus) hath ouerflowed thy banks and thy buildings (ô thou glory of Great Brittaine) and made thee fertile (for many yeeres together) in all kindes of Vices? Volga, that hath fifty streames falling one into another, neuer ranne with so swift and unresistable a current as these Black-waters do, to bring vpon thee an Inundation.

If thou (as thou hast done) kneelest to worship this Beast with Seuen Crowned Heads, and the Whore that sits vpon it, the fall of thee (that hast out-stood so many

Citties) will be greater then that of Babylon. She is now gotten within thy walls; she rides vp and downe thy streetes, making thee drunke out of her cup, and marking thee in the forhead with pestilence for her owne. She causes Violls of wrath to be powred vpon thee, and goes in triumph away, when she sees thee falling. If thou wilt be safe therefore and recouer health, rise vp in Armes against her, and driue her (and the Monster that beares her) out at thy Gates. Thou seest how prowdly and impetuously sixe of these Centuares (that are halfe man, halfe beast, and halfe diuell) come thundring alongst thy Habitations, and what rabbles they bring at their heeles; take now but note of the last, and marke how the seuenth rides: for if thou findest but the least worthy quality in any one of them to make thee loue him, I will write a Retractation of what is inueyd against them before, and pollish such an Apology in their defence, that thou shalt be enamored of them all.

The body and face of this Tyrannous Commander, that leades thus the Reareward, are already drawne: his Chariot is framed all of ragged Flint so artificially bestowed, that as it runnes, they strike one another, and beate out fire that is able to consume Citties: the wheeles are many, and swift: the Spokes of the wheeles, are the Shinbones of wretches that haue bin eaten by misery out of prison. A couple of vnruly, fierce, and vntamed Tygers (cald Murder and Rashnes) drew the Chariot: Ignorance holds the reynes of the one, and Obduration of the other: Selfe-will is the Coachman. In the vpper end of the Coach, sits Cruelty alone, vpon a bench made of dead mens sculls. All the way that he rides, he sucks the hearts of widdowes and father-lesse children. He keepes neither foote-men nor Pages, for none will stay long with him. He hath onely one attendant that euer followes him, called Repentance, but the Beast that drawes him, runnes away with his good Lord and Master so fast before, that Repentance being lame (and therefore slow) tis alwayes very late ere he comes to him. It is to be feared, that Cruelty is of great authority where he is knowne, for few or none dare stand against him: Law only now and then beards him, and stayes him, in contempt of those that so terribly gallop before him; but out of the Lawes hands, if he can but snatch a sheathed sword (as oftentimes hee

does) presently hee whips it out, smiting and wounding with it euery one that giues him the least crosse word. He comes into the Citty, commonly at All-gate, beeing drawne that way by the smell of bloud about the Barres, (for by his good will he drinks no other liquor:) but when hee findes it to be the bloud of Beasts (amongst the Butchers) and not of men, he flyes like lightning along the Causey in a madnes, threatning to ouer-runne all whom he meetes: but spying the Brokers of Hownsditch shuffling themselues so long together (like a false paire of Cards) till the Knaues be vppermost, onely to doe homage to him, he stops, kissing all their cheekes, calling them all his deerest Sonnes; and bestowing a damnable deale of his blessing vpon them, they cry, Roome for Cruelty, and are the onely men that bring him into the Citty:
To follow whom vp and downe so farre
as they meane to goe with him,

—Dii me terrent, & Iupiter hostis.

FINIS.

Tho. Dekker.

www.ingramcontent.com/pod-product-compliance
Ingram Content Group UK Ltd.
Pitfield, Milton Keynes, MK11 3LW, UK
UKHW042150280225
455719UK00001B/246